M000014580

Pedro Arrupe SJ

MYSTIC WITH OPEN EYES

With an Introduction by Peter McVerry SJ

BRIAN GROGAN SJ

First published in 2019 by Messenger Publications

The material in this publication is protected by copyright law.
Except as may be permitted by law, no part of the material may
be reproduced (including by storage in a retrieval system) or transmitted
in any form or by any means, adapted, rented or lent without the written
permission of the copyright owners. Applications for permissions
should be addressed to the publisher.

The right of Brian Grogan SJ to be identified as the
author of the Work has been asserted by him in accordance with the
Copyright and Related Rights Act, 2000.

ISBN 978 1 78812 024 1

Copyright © Brian Grogan, 2019

Designed by Messenger Publications Design Department
Typeset in Times New Roman and Charlemagne Std
Printed by Nicholson & Bass Ltd

Messenger Publications,
37 Lower Leeson Street, Dublin 2
www.messenger.ie

DEDICATION

To those in great cities and on the peripheries, who find in Ignatian spirituality the inspiration and courage to labour for a civilisation of love.

ACKNOWLEDGEMENTS

This booklet could not have been written without constant reference to Kevin Burke's *Pedro Arrupe: Essential Writings*. (New York: Orbis, 2004), and to Gianni La Bella's *Pedro Arrupe: New Contributions for his Biography* (Bilbao: Ediciones Mensajero, 2007). To both scholars my sincere thanks.

FOREWORD

I entered the Jesuit novitiate in 1962. It might just as well have been 1862: a life dominated by rules, to be observed without questioning, cut off from an outside world which was full of temptations. Our community was our castle, a safe place to which we would return after venturing out to minister to the faithful.

Then came Pedro Arrupe. I met him twice in Dublin and his presence and talks reflected a deep peace that clearly derived from a strong belief in God's love and providence. He was a very charismatic person, a true prophet.

Perhaps it was his experience of ministering to the survivors of Hiroshima and reflecting on the appalling injustice of inflicting such pain on innocent civilians that brought him to believe that our faith in God impels us to reach out to the suffering and the poor and to challenge those structures that keep so many in poverty and exclusion. He set out a new vision for the Jesuits, a vision that identified the promotion of justice in our world as the defining characteristic of every Jesuit ministry and of the work of every Jesuit.

The Irish Jesuit response to this new mission was to send some Jesuits into the inner city of Dublin to live and work. I was privileged to be one of them. This changed my life and the life of the Irish Province for ever. Perhaps, like Pedro Arrupe, it was the first-hand experience of suffering and poverty that changed me. There was a lot of opposition to this mission from some other Jesuits. The

Province, like the wider Society, went through a time of change that was difficult, controversial and sometimes divisive. But there was no turning back.

Eventually, the opposition – trained to be obedient Jesuits! – embraced this new mission, albeit with some reluctance. Every Jesuit ministry in Ireland was asked to reflect on if, and how, it was serving the poor and promoting justice and to adapt accordingly. Several more communities in disadvantaged areas were established. Pedro Arrupe's conviction that working for justice was central to living the Gospel set the Society of Jesus, and the Irish Province, on a clear and firm path into the future which continues to this day.

Peter McVerry SJ.

CHAPTER 1

'GO!'

I was invited in late 1981 to go to Somalia. My poor knowledge of geography forced me to search for Somalia on the map: it is not exactly a holiday resort. The communist authorities had expelled nearly all priests in 1974 and seven years on someone was needed, I was told, to find out how they would react to an incoming priest. It would be an opportunity too, I was told, to do some field-work for the Jesuit Refugee Service (JRS) which had been inaugurated by Pedro Arrupe (1907-1991), Superior General of the Jesuits, in 1980. Since the plane for Mogadishu was to leave from Rome, I went there and was invited to visit Pedro: it was to be my sixth and final meeting with him, because some months earlier he had suffered a devastating stroke that was to render him ever more incapacitated for the final decade of his life.

In the darkened room in which he was convalescing I explained where and why I was going. His eyes lit up: he half raised himself from the couch, stuck out a trembling arm at me and shouted 'Go!' Go I did, and his command carried me through some scary times. His single word 'Go!' still energises me: I think of him, with his tiny frail body and broad smile, as a man in whom the Holy Spirit had unrestricted freedom to operate, and sometimes I pray to him to give me a little share of his limitless freedom and availability to God. I have asked his help in writing these pages.

His speech of acceptance when he was elected in 1965 began with the words of Jeremiah, who in about 600BC was called to be a prophet of God: '"Ah, ah, ah, Lord, I do not know how to speak … But God said, "You shall go to all to whom I send you, and you shall speak whatever I command you"' (Jer 1:6–7). *'You shall go'*: it seems to me that he himself was always trying to listen to the Spirit and coaxing others, like myself, to do likewise. No one shaped my life more than he, because he radically reshaped and reenergised the Society of Jesus that I had joined eleven years earlier.

Pedro was a tiny man with a great heart. Never threatening or dominating, he was always welcoming, and when he looked at you with his big eyes you knew there was space in his heart for you. He was transparent; the good Spirit shone out through him. In referring to Jesus, Pedro uses the term 'luminous transcendence' and the same could be applied to him. He radiated an inner glow, and as I begin to write I think of him, not simply as a fascinating figure in the past, but as glowing within the body of humanity. If, as contemporary science assures us, all things are interconnected, surely those who have gone ahead of us and who have become fully themselves, energise the rest of us and exercise a hidden influence on our development.

My use of the term 'Pedro' is to be taken to indicate the affectionate respect which so many people had for him. He was often called 'Don Pedro'.

Heart to Heart

It is important from the outset to emphasise what made him tick, lest we get lost in his struggles and achievements and miss the 'secret scripture' of his long life. From early on he seems to have had a strong and intimate relationship with God.

This is revealed in his writings, for instance when he was commending devotion to the Sacred Heart. Picking up on the word 'heart', he describes it as a *primary* word, packed with meaning and sentiment. For him it expressed the fundamental reality of being in love with the Person of Christ who was already fully in love with him. 'It could be said that every line of the Gospel, every word of it, is throbbing with the boundless love of Christ, who is burning with love for every human being.'

Jesus is already what Pedro wishes to become; not just a historical figure 'out there' to be imitated and admired; nor to be found only in the Church and the Eucharist. 'He dwells in the innermost depths of our heart.' This presence is 'something of our own intimate being – within us, close to us, our heart's treasure. So we can speak with Jesus heart to heart: we can listen to one another, feel for one another'. This gives a hint of his lived prayerful experience. He prays: 'Give me that grace, that sense of you, your very heartbeat.'

Elsewhere he comments: 'Nowadays the world does not need words, but lives which cannot be explained except through faith and love for Christ poor'. This is the heart of the man.

God's world

Pedro Arrupe is becoming recognised as one of the towering figures of the twentieth century. His life touched all of its decades: he was seven when the First World War broke out, was expelled from Spain with his fellow Jesuits in 1931, reached Japan in 1938, lived through the Second World War, including Pearl Harbour, and played his part in alleviating the savage torture that the first atomic bomb wreaked on Hiroshima. He knew of the Holocaust, the Cold War and the MAD era – the time of Mutually Assured Destruction. He lived through the endless regional conflicts and periodic genocides that littered the last century. None of this was lost on him but instead shaped his perspectives. The range of his concerns was limitless, because he saw our world as God's world. He had a prophetic gift to offer in response to the tragedies of humankind, and he shaped the lives of many, both Jesuit and other, with an optimism and vision that was in no way naïve but based on the belief that the Lord still cares for his people and welcomes generous hearts to help them in their deepest needs. He accepted the risk of intimacy with God.

Mystic with open eyes

He has been referred to as the second founder of the Jesuits because he donned the mantle of Ignatius and reclaimed the original charism of the Jesuits in the light of the Second Vatican Council (1962-65). More profoundly he has been described as 'a mystic with open eyes' because he gazed on our messy world as God does, on the world of the atom bomb, of expulsions, refugees, imprisonments, tortures, world wars, poverty, clashes of ideologies. He would say: 'See with the eyes of Christ, go wherever the need is greatest, serve the faith and promote justice as best you can, and you will find God!' In Ignatian terminology, he was truly a *contemplative in action*: he looked at the world in all its joys and sorrows and tried to discern how God might want him and his Order to respond to its needs.

I met him in our house in Dublin in 1977 and opened the conversation by asking how things were moving along. His face lit up, and he said, 'On the one hand everything is wonderful … On the other hand, things are not so good!' There is the mystic with open eyes, neither lost in an otherworldly spirituality nor cynical about the state of the world. With one of his aides he would sing the spiritual, 'Nobody knows the trouble I've seen' – which he jokingly referred to as his theme song – but he had an unquestioning conviction that God is everywhere at work, orchestrating the chaos of human affairs. While he never referred to himself as a mystic, he prayed to have the eyes of a mystic: 'Grant me, O Lord, to see everything now with *new eyes*. Give me the clarity of understanding that you gave St Ignatius.'

He has left behind him a small library of writings and addresses and influenced many religious congregations, whose members in turn have touched the hearts of innumerable lay persons. Who can say how many have inherited his legacy and are generously living out his dream? His vision and enthusiasm for humankind have become embedded in Catholic thinking.

Now that his cause for beatification has been introduced, a vast project is underway to gather all that is known about him. This booklet is being written while that project is still in germination: the sketch given here will be filled out in years to come. At the end of each chapter I offer a reflection to help you to bring the richness of Pedro's story to bear on the shaping of your own. As his successor, Peter-Hans Kolvenbach said, 'He no longer belongs to Jesuits only. He belongs to the whole Church. Indeed he belongs to the whole world.'

For Reflection

Mary Oliver asks in her poem, *The Summer Day*: 'Tell me, what is it you plan to do with your one wild and precious life?'

Does the above outline of Pedro's life throw any light on your own? What might you learn from him to help you shape 'your one wild and precious life'?

CHAPTER 2

ON A GIANT'S SHOULDERS

'We are like dwarves sitting on the shoulders of giants. We see more, and see more distant things than they did because they raise us up and by their great stature add to ours'. This observation of a twelfth century theologian fits Pedro: he did not emerge out of the blue. His life's orientation had its human roots in the founder of the Jesuits, Ignatius of Loyola (1491–1556) of whom there are many excellent studies. Here we note only a few of Ignatius' characteristics which shaped the mind and heart of the young Basque Pedro in the 1920s.

Led by Another

Ignatius made an unpromising start: he was a wastrel, a brawler, a womaniser. He was fool-hardy but also imaginative, determined and chivalrous. At the age of thirty his dreams were shattered through a war-injury and over long months of convalescence he found himself battling with two desires: one the service of a noble lady by whose beauty he had been smitten; the other the service of Jesus with whom he found himself falling in love as he read the Gospels on his sick bed. It took him months to notice that while both possibilities engrossed him, the first left him dissatisfied and unfulfilled, whereas the after-glow of the other continued to warm and nourish his heart even when he turned to other things. His interpretation was that the sustaining consolation came 'from above' and was God's preferred way of pointing the way forward for him. This, he tells us, was his first exercise in the art of the discernment of spirits: he yielded to it and became, in the happy phrase of a recent biographer, 'a man led by Another'.

He became a pilgrim, limping with his bad leg along the rough roads of Europe, educating himself so that he could help people in their spiritual growth and writing a little book of spiritual exercises built up from personal experience and reading. He gathered companions, lost them but found others and with them founded the Society of Jesus – the Jesuits – in 1540. He spent the last sixteen years of his life governing this Society, always on the search for what greater service it might give to God. He left his mark on the world and the Church and continues to do so through his spirituality, which is centred on the conviction that God has dreams for each of us which we can come to know and joyously fulfil.

The magis

One Ignatian keyword is 'magis', (Latin for *'more'*). An umbrella term, it catches up the dynamism of the medieval code of chivalry and refers to the desire to do the best one can with one's life and talents. The Ignatian *magis* involves the sublimation of one's best desires and talents for the service of God and the world. Those imbued with the *magis* see God as ever-active, labouring in the world and inviting them into collaboration. Followers of Ignatius are meant to live out of an awesome grace that tilts them towards seeing the world with the eyes of Christ, loving it with his heart and serving it with his compassion. Then, contemplation and action fuse into one, as they did in Jesus and they can say with him, 'I always do what pleases my Father' (Jn 8:29).

Help people!

Ignatius developed this single aim in life – to help others. What could be simpler or more concrete? The history of the Jesuits is remarkable, turbulent, complex, contradictory but imagine a band of people who had no other aim than to be of service to those in need. Anything is possible for them, if they follow the promptings of the good Spirit. As good golfers try to keep their eye on the ball whether it's lying on the fairway, in the rough or in the bunker, Ignatius recommended his men to try to *keep God always before their eyes*, no matter in what difficulties they found themselves. They would need discerning hearts as they edged their way along in an uncharted and changing world. Faced with any new situation, Ignatius would have his followers ask 'what ought we to do? What would give God greater glory?' 'The greater glory of God' thus became the Jesuit motto, and Ignatius and his companions called themselves 'Companions of Jesus'.

As a young man Pedro was captivated by these ideals. It seems to have been easy for him to dedicate himself to God and to identify with Jesus and his world-vision. We see the *magis* operating throughout his life: his choice for God's service which entailed abandoning medical studies and a prestigious career, his desire to go to the ends of the earth to serve in Japan, his heroic response to the havoc of Hiroshima, his taking on the burden of leading 36,000 men into an uncertain future after the Second Vatican Council, his freedom in wanting to relinquish his role when he felt no longer able to sustain it, his remaining cheerful and positive through the dark and empty years of his final illness.

Next we will turn to Pedro himself.

For Reflection

Do you notice a touch of chivalry in yourself, an outward-bound quality? How does the aim of 'helping others' appeal to you? If this is what your life is already about, thank God for that.

Do you believe that you are unique and that God loves and respects your uniqueness?

CHAPTER 3

FORMATIVE YEARS 1907-38

Born on 14 November 1907 in Bilbao, Northern Spain, Pedro Arrupe, like Ignatius, was a Basque. The family was a happy one; he had four sisters, older than himself, so he was treated with great affection. This helps us to understand his joyous, optimistic and loving personality which was to be so tested later. Sadly his mother died when he was nine, and his father passed away when he was twenty, but they had seen to it that he got the best available Catholic education. He lived in a Catholic atmosphere, and it seems that he never came to doubt his faith. A bright student, he loved theatre, music, opera. Sensitive and idealistic, he was captivated by the desire to heal people, so he studied medicine, and a brilliant career was in prospect for him.

The tugs of God

In 1926 he went to Lourdes for three months and worked with the Bureau that investigated reported cures. He verified two cures, and his comment was: 'I sensed God very close and tugging at me'.

He attributed the concretising of his vocation to being present at a cure. The Blessed Sacrament was being brought around to the waiting invalids. Pedro continues:

> A young man of around twenty was there, all twisted and contorted by polio. His mother was reciting the rosary in a loud voice and from time to time would sigh, 'Maria santisima, help us'. The moment came when the bishop was to bless the young man with the host. The man looked at the host with the same faith with which the paralytic in the Gospel must have looked at Jesus. After the bishop had made the sign of the Cross with the Blessed Sacrament, the young man rose cured from the cart, and the crowd, filled with joy, cried out: 'Miracle! Miracle!'

> I had been an eyewitness of a true miracle worked by Jesus Christ in the Eucharist! I was filled with an immense joy: I seemed to be standing by the side of Jesus, and as I sensed his almighty power the world around me began to appear extremely small ... Three months later, in 1927, I entered the novitiate of the Society of Jesus in Loyola, Spain.

His sense of the closeness of God is of critical importance to understanding what went on in him and sustained him throughout his long life. It was present in his joys and sorrows, his achievements and failures. He would have made his own the insight of Teilhard de Chardin SJ, his contemporary: 'By means of all created things, without exception, the divine assails us, penetrates and moulds us. We imagined it as distant and inaccessible, when in fact we live steeped in its burning layers'. From a monastic vantage point Thomas Merton came to the same awareness, in his *New Seeds of Contemplation* he notes: 'Every moment and every event in every person's life plants seeds of spiritual vitality in their soul'. Awareness of this extraordinary closeness of God in every detail of life is rare, but it is life-changing, even if disconcerting and sometimes uncomfortable!

Early on, Pedro asked to be sent to Japan, where Francis Xavier had laboured almost four centuries earlier. He was told to wait. In 1932 the Order was expelled from Spain by the government of the new Republic. All Jesuit property was seized, and 2,700 Jesuits had to seek refuge elsewhere in Europe. This was a shattering experience of disruption and of injustice and raised for Pedro issues that shaped his perspective of the Church by the secular world, an issue that shaped his perspective for the remainder of his life.

Pedro found a home among the Belgian Jesuits, where he continued his studies in philosophy, this was followed by the study of theology in the Netherlands with the German Jesuits. In 1936 he was ordained and sent to Kansas in the US to complete his studies. He concluded his Jesuit training with a year of spiritual formation in Cleveland, Ohio.

Why Japan?

He was finally missioned to Japan in 1938. Why did he want to go there? He said himself that his only missionary motive was God's will.

> During my annual retreat in 1929 [less than two years after joining the Jesuits] I had a clear vision that my vocation was to be a missionary and that it would lead me to Japan. And don't ask me what

'vision' means: it's a question of an intimate experience that no word can describe and that can only be understood as it unfolds in time.

He believed that the tension between our smallness and the creator's greatness

runs like a master thread through each person's history … each of us carries a personal secret that not even they fully understand. It is the area of closest relationship between God who loves each one in a different way, and the human being who from the depths of their being gives a response that is unique because there is not nor will there ever be their like.

Trinitarian love, he said, irrupts into our lives and is wonderfully decisive. He is speaking for himself here, expressing the *magis*, the 'more' that fuelled his spirit. He concludes simply: 'I have the impression that my life is written in a single sentence: "It has unfolded according to the will of God"'.

He sailed from Seattle and arrived in Yokahama two weeks later. He studied Japanese in Nagatsuka, near Hiroshima, but while he spoke six other languages, he was not a linguist. Someone commented that he actually spoke Spanish in seven languages! He once played his fiddle in a Yamaguchi square to gather an audience, much as Xavier had done 400 years earlier when he rang his bell. We don't know whether either initiative was an apostolic triumph or not!

Solitary Confinement

Shortly after the Japanese attack on Pearl Harbour in December 1941 and America's entry into the Second World

War, he was arrested as an American spy, and spent thirty-three days in prison and solitary confinement. Deprived of the Eucharist and of all human comfort, he says:

> I experienced this deep pain for the lack of the Eucharist, but there was at the same time a feeling of the faithful and consoling presence of our Lord. What loneliness there was: I then appreciated what the Eucharist means to a priest, to a Jesuit, for whom the Mass and the tabernacle are the very centre of his life. I believe that this was the month that I learned the most in all my life.

He had time to contemplate the possibility of tortures such as many of his brethren had endured before him. They are graphically depicted in Martin Scorsese's 2016 film, *Silence*. He prayed for courage and found God close. 'It was beautiful, the solitude with Christ, a mystical experience, nothing in my cell, only me and Christ'.

His eyes would fill with tears in telling this story. Again, as with his expulsion with his brethren from Spain he had here a direct experience of personal injustice since he, a Spaniard, had offered his life simply to bring the Good News to the people of Japan. He began to ponder how the message of Christ could ever be heard above the din of hatred and violence.

Interrogated for an unbroken thirty-six hours, he found himself astonished that the Spirit of wisdom prompted his replies, as promised by Jesus to his disciples (Mk 13:11). Again there is that sense of divine closeness, even in the depths of pain and misery. On Christmas night his spirits sank low: it seemed rather to be Good Friday! Then he began to hear a soft murmuring outside his cell and wondered what it might mean.

There arose a soft, sweet, consoling Christmas carol, one which I myself had taught my Christians. I burst into tears. Heedless of the danger of being themselves imprisoned, they had come to console me. It lasted for a few minutes, and then there was silence again: they had gone and I was left to myself. But I felt that Jesus had descended into my heart, and that night I made the best spiritual communion of my life.

For Reflection

Do you ever feel God close and tugging at you, perhaps not as an irruption but as a gentle invitation?

If you do not as yet experience that you are 'led by Another' can this become material for your prayer?

CHAPTER 4

HIROSHIMA, 1945

Freed from prison, Pedro in 1942 was put in charge of Japanese novices. While he was preparing these starving young men to serve the spiritual needs of their people, in the United States the Manhattan Project – the creation of the atom bomb – was under way at immense cost. On the Feast of the Transfiguration, 6 August 1945, while homilies across the world carried a message of hope for the future of humanity and spoke of divine fire descending from heaven, the A-bomb was dropped on the unsuspecting city of Hiroshima. It fell to earth with a blinding flash, a crashing thunder, a devastating blast and a deceptively beautiful mushroom cloud. And it changed the history of humankind.

On that fateful day Pedro was living on the outskirts of Hiroshima in the town of Nagatsuka. He wrote a dramatic account of what happened after 08.15.

There was a blinding flash, a huge explosion, and

then doors, windows and walls fell on us in smithereens. No one was injured. Not knowing what had happened, we climbed a hill and saw below the ruins of Hiroshima. Japanese houses were made of wood, paper and straw, breakfast was being prepared, so when flames and electric current met, the entire city became one enormous lake of fire.

Pedro and his men felt helpless: they knelt and prayed, then decided to make their house into a field hospital. Torrents of rain helped to dampen the fires, and after twelve hours they were able to enter the destroyed city. They squeezed 150 wounded into their small house, and using his medical skills Pedro sorted out the patients into various groups. Many had been burnt by flames, others developed huge blisters. No one at that moment knew what caused these; only later they realised they were the after-effect of infrared radiation.

Two hundred children perished in one school when the roof collapsed on them: hundreds of others were left searching for their parents. The limbs of many victims were calcified. A person sitting on a flight of stone stairs outside a bank was instantly incinerated, but not without leaving a lasting mark: the surface of the steps was turned white and the place where the person had been sitting became a shadow on the stone. Many of the wounded had fled to the river to escape burning, but when the tide came in they were half-buried in mud and so died by drowning.

Pedro used his office desk as an operating table. The suffering of victims was frightful but there was not a word of complaint. A young married man whose body was a running sore kept repeating, 'Father, don't hesitate to hurt me; I can take it, but just save me'. He and his faithful wife stayed eight months and were finally able to resume their lives. Some parents found their children alive and living with the Jesuits, and threw themselves at their feet in wordless gratitude.

Thus it was that Pedro had led the first rescue party into the doomed city. He had brought home scarred human beings to the Jesuit house, human beings who had been burned, boiled, skinned, deafened, blinded but who were survivors of what only later was recognised as an atomic bomb: a new term had entered the world's vocabulary. He said later: 'We were in effect the first guinea pigs in this experimentation'. The little band had been warned by the authorities: 'Do not enter the city: there is a gas in the air that will kill people for the next seventy years'. But they went in and helped to cremate 50,000 bodies and care for at least a few of the 120,000 wounded. Pedro often spoke about the experience when travelling the world in the search for personnel and funding for the Japanese mission. For him the bomb was 'a mystery of iniquity, a permanent experience outside of history, engraved on my memory'. Again came the questions that would not go away: 'Where is God in all this, and what should be the role of the Church and the Jesuits in the face of such horrors?'

If we ask what made Pedro respond as he did, an Ignatian theme suggests the answer. In his Spiritual Exercises Ignatius has the retreatant question his crucified Lord, 'What ought I do?' Whenever a need emerges, God may want help. So it was for Pedro that fateful day: instead of celebrating spiritually the Transfiguration of Jesus, he felt called to go into the ravaged city to help those whose lives had been destroyed.

Superior in Japan

Life continued for Pedro in a broken nation, and in 1954 he was appointed vice-Provincial to continue the task of evangelisation. It was difficult work: towards the close of his active life he remarked when encouraging his brethren who were working in Thailand:

> You see little success externally in a country that is mostly Buddhist and where there are so few Catholics. I think I can speak from experience! In Japan you may find a parish priest baptising only two people in ten years. What is in question here is not external success but commitment.

In 1958 Japan became a full province, and he was named provincial, a post he held till he left for a fateful Jesuit gathering in Rome in 1965. An indomitable traveller, in that time he circled the globe several times, and under his guidance the Japanese Province reached a membership of 300 Jesuits gathered from some thirty countries.

For Reflection

A bomb can fall under many forms: an unexpected death or illness, a tragedy afflicting someone else, an unjust situation … Can you identify such events in your own life?

We have seen how Pedro responded even with limited resources. How do you respond to difficult situations? Do you ask the Lord, 'What ought I do?'

CHAPTER 5

SUPERIOR GENERAL, 1965

As the youngest Jesuit teacher in St Ignatius College Galway on the 22 May 1965, I had the task of reading out to the community at dinner Pedro Arrupe's acceptance speech on his election as Superior General. He was fifty-eight, and the twenty-eighth superior general of an Order that had 36,000 men. It was a moment of high emotion for us.

He had come to Rome as an outsider for the thirty-first Jesuit General Congregation; he was a humble missionary from the ends of the earth, who had tried only to convince his brethren that the Society of Jesus must adapt radically to meet the needs of the contemporary world. His listeners were impressed, and they already knew him from his travels on behalf of the Japanese mission. On the positive side were his age and health, his boundless zeal, his capacity for inculturation, his ability to effect change, his gift for easy and trusting relationships, his knowledge of the Society and his linguistic ability. He had been tried in the inferno of Hiroshima and had not been found wanting. On the negative side qualities mentioned were an excessive idealism, a naïvete shown in being over-trusting, poor capacity for overall strategy and organisation.

As we have noted he began his speech of acceptance with the line from Jeremiah about being unable to speak. He went on:

> These words express my feeling of smallness. It is however evident that God's will has done this. 'Do not be afraid, for I am with you.' I have never felt before so intimately our Lord's word: 'Cut off from me you can do nothing'. Still, since the choice came from God, I can still say in humility with St Paul: 'There is nothing I cannot master with the help of the one who gives me strength'.

Jesuit Renewal

Pedro was articulate, incisive, comprehensive, intelligible and soon became the darling of the media. He had the gift of commending tough ideals in a persuasive way, at least to those who had a spirit of openness and generosity. His radiant smile invited a positive response from those with whom he was speaking. For sixteen turbulent years he spearheaded the renewal of the Jesuits and and as President of the Union of Superiors General he influenced all other congregations of Ignatian inspiration. His first task was to preside over the general congregation which had elected him. No congregation achieved more: every aspect of Jesuit life was scrutinised to bring it into line both with the original Ignatian charism and the demands of the Vatican Council which was just ending.

More than 400 years of lived Jesuit history had to be

focused towards the new world that was emerging. It was not surprising that strong divergences of view emerged that were hard to reconcile. Pedro's leadership was clear, encouraging, honest as he faced the mountainous task of renewal and rejuvenation. One of his remarks was, 'Even if the pilot can't see the port, that's OK!' Often asked, 'Where is the Society heading?' he would reply with a twinkle in his eyes, 'Where God is leading it'. The pope, Paul VI, maintained a watchful oversight on the congregation, not hesitating to criticise those Jesuits who were neglecting their interior lives or were difficult to govern. Reports by some bishops caused him concern: some Jesuits, they said, seemed to be abandoning essential elements of the Order in favour of a secular mentality. Not all criticisms were wide of the mark.

Hence he had the task of recovering the essence of Ignatian spirituality and commending it across the Society. It had developed accretions over the centuries and had become regimented, governed by bell and rule-book. Imagination had become stultified in a cramping environment. He used the image of men stuck in concrete who must be set free to become again pliable instruments in the divine hands.

He encouraged a more personal style of authority, supportive of personal freedom and responsibility but demanding inner growth and openness to the challenges set by contemporary needs.

In the search for a common identity amid its vast diversity, Pedro recovered for the Society the Spiritual Exercises of St Ignatius. He also distinguished Ignatian spirituality from Jesuit spirituality; the former is a gift for any and all, while the latter refers to the Order alone.

Desolation?

Pedro sometimes spoke of a state of desolation among not a few Jesuits, due to hierarchical criticism, departures and fewer vocations. Numbers were dropping by a thousand men annually. There was also a certain loss of common identity, strong internal divisions and a querying of the value of religious life in the light of the Second Vatican Council's universal call to holiness. The insight was that you don't have to be a religious to be pleasing to God! Many took the plunge and left.

In regard to mission he articulated his fears about the value of the Order to a needy world:

> I am afraid that we Jesuits may have little or nothing to offer this new world, little or nothing to say or do that would justify our existence as Jesuits. I am afraid that we may repeat yesterday's answers to tomorrow's problems, and talk in a language that does not speak to the heart. Then we shall be left speaking to ourselves.

Thus the early years of his leadership flew by, with careful preparation of talks and letters, followed by large meetings and intense debate everywhere he went. His incisive comments, his sincerity and enthusiasm, were infectious and encouraging especially to those labouring on the peripheries.

For Reflection

Can you name your limitations as well as your strengths?
Do you believe that human weakness, if acknowledged,
allows God to work freely?

CHAPTER 6

SEA-CHANGES, 1965–ONWARD

Corporate discernment came into prominence as Jesuits and their associates engaged in serious and prayerful evaluation of the new needs God might be asking them to serve. Choice of living-place was to be decided by choice of ministry. They reminded themselves of the statement of one of their founding members: 'We are not monks: the world is our home'. Mobility began to re-assert itself: remote houses of formation were abandoned in favour of urban locations, guided by the awareness that whereas St Benedict loved the heights and St Bernard the valleys, Ignatius loved the great cities. Space here allows the mention of only a few apostolic works which underwent radical change.

Education
In response to the charge that he was downgrading education in favour of direct work with the poor, Pedro in

1970 proposed education as one of the top four priorities for the Society. In 1973 he gave an address to the Tenth International Congress of Jesuit Alumni in Europe.

> Probably no address I ever made has been so widely circulated or had greater influence in the Society and outside it. True, there were those who hated it, and those who loved it. The President of the Spanish Alumni resigned in protest, and in many places it was said that the Jesuits had gone communist! I knew my message would offend some in high places, but I felt I had to speak as bluntly as I did.

The original title of the talk was 'Men for Others': this he later emended to 'Men and Women for Others'. More recently the slogan has become 'Men and women for and with others'. What were the ideas that caused such a stir? Pedro stated unequivocally that the prime Jesuit educational objective must be to form men and women for others, persons who cannot even conceive of a love for God that does not include love for those less well-off than themselves. He acknowledged that in this area the Jesuits had failed their alumni: conversion of heart was needed if they were to come to the aid of a humankind that is oppressed and in agony. A basic attitude of respect for everyone was needed; a resolve never to dominate the weak and a willingness to resist all forms of injustice. Sin, he said, is not 'neat'. It is not simply a blemish on the soul but reaches into us to infect us deeply. It can poison our thinking, our behavioural patterns, our cultural structures and eventually can dehumanise us. This is why Christ comes to redeem not only the individual heart but the culture, the systems, institutions and structures that confine our lives and restrict our God-given freedom for good. We are to win back not only our whole selves but our whole world for God. This is why, he continued, Christian education is a call to conversion, to become fully human by growing in love for other humans.

Reading this long address forty-five years on still makes me gasp: perhaps each succeeding generation has to grapple with its challenges anew. For some, as for the disciples who walked away from Jesus, it was 'impossible teaching – who can accept it?' In exchange for an exclusive image of Jesuit education Pedro was offering one that was radically inclusive.

Racial equality

A letter to American Jesuits was direct and practical. He praised the work of individual Jesuits but required that as a body they should ask, 'Why so little of our effort in the past has been expended in work for and with black people?' He stipulated that Jesuit houses were to be opened in poor areas; young Jesuits should experience the practical problems of the inner city and of racial discrimination.

This was his style: he was never abrasive but was certainly forthright in expressing what should be done. He called things by their name. Inevitably some local Church authorities opposed moves of this kind, which led to frustration in the Order at not being allowed to meet the real needs of the poor, as proposed by the Second Vatican Council. It was claimed, not entirely unfairly, that some Jesuits were forging ahead, claiming that they had 'the spirit of Vatican II' and in the process becoming a parallel but disobedient Church.

Humanae Vitae, Pope Paul's 1968 Encyclical on birth control, caused difficultiues for many good people in the practice of their Catholic faith. While Arrupe asked his men for loyal obedience around the Encyclical he insisted that 'to obey is not to stop thinking, nor to parrot the Encyclical word for word in a servile manner'. This must have given the Vatican matter for thought: what did the Jesuit general really mean?

For Reflection

Would you describe yourself as being 'for and with others', especially for the disadvantaged?

'What ought I do?' Do you sometimes know what to do, but lack the energy to do it? At this point do you ask God's help?

CHAPTER 7

A MAN OF PRAYER

The more you have to do, the more you need to pray! This is a slogan of the spiritual tradition, born of experience. On my wall is my favourite portrait of Pedro: he is black-gowned, seated in a zen-like posture, absorbed in silent prayer. His sandals are beside him, a symbol of the fact that for this sacred time he is not on the move: no matter how pressing his affairs, this quality time is being given over to God alone.

How long?
He believed so deeply in God that he was drawn to spend long hours daily in silent prayer; he slept only about four hours at night. A novice once asked him, 'How much time to you give to prayer, Father?' He launched into a little homily on the importance of prayer for a Jesuit. But the novice was brave, and insisted: 'How many hours do *you* pray every day?' Silence, then the reply, 'About four

hours'. More silence. Then he added, 'But in that time I also offer Mass and say part of the Divine Office. And of course, one needs to be talking with God all the time. Isn't that what Ignatius says?' One of my brethren was living next to our visitor's room when Pedro showed up. Knowing the story about the four hours' prayer, he decided not to let the Irish Province down, so he set his alarm for four o'clock, ran the taps noisily, got back into bed and woke up in time for breakfast!

In writing the Jesuit *Constitutions* in the 1540s, Ignatius lays out with charming simplicity how the general should spend his day: partly with God, partly with his staff and partly with himself in deciding what should be done with God's help. God is mentioned first! So in a twelve-hour day prayer might well occupy four hours. Pedro took this to heart; he called the small chapel in his apartments his little cathedral and loved to withdraw there.

As for 'talking with God all the time' he had made his own Ignatius's discovery that God can be found in our feelings and moods, our likes and dislikes. God, he saw, is at play in our inner world, and by stopping off periodically in the day to notice what is going on inside, we can track the path of the Spirit: thus we learn where we are being led. Ignatius developed a spirituality of the heart which helps people to seek and find God in the world around them. Under pressure from an insistent biographer in the final phase of his life, he confessed that 'he was always growing in ease in finding God, and every time and hour he wanted to find God, he found him'. This was true of Pedro too: his waking hours seem to have been immersed in the divine. He was truly contemplative, in action as well as in his formal times of prayer.

The Eucharist

In his devotion to the Eucharist he also resembled Ignatius, who would often take two hours to celebrate. We have noted that when in solitary confinement for thirty-three days in a Japanese prison, his greatest suffering was to be deprived of the Eucharist, which was, he states, the centre of his life, 'the most important act of the entire daily routine'. I recall how upset he became when some younger Jesuits began to question the value of daily Eucharist. 'Wouldn't weekly Eucharist suffice?' they asked. He found their arguments hard to understand, since for himself this daily meeting with God was his spirit's life-blood. One of his Benedictine friends acknowledged that while Pedro wouldn't get high grades for liturgical awareness, his sense of the transcendent always shone through. At his Masses one knew a holy man was presiding.

Mass on Mount Fujiyama

Not only was the Eucharist important to him personally, but it had for him a cosmic significance. Shortly after his arrival in Japan in 1938, Pedro and a Jesuit brother climbed Fujiyama, Japan's sacred mountain. A hard climb of 11,000 feet, it had to be done by four in the morning, since by six the peak would be covered in cloud. He described what happened:

> My mind was bubbling with projects for the conversion of the whole of Japan. The climb had been most tiring, but at the top the sight of the rising sun was stupendous. Above us was the blue sky, below us 80 million people who did not know God. My mind ranged out beyond the lofty vaulting of the sky to the seat of the Blessed Trinity. I seemed

to see Jesus and with him St Francis Xavier, the first apostle of Japan, whose hair had become white within a few months because of the sufferings he had endured. If I had known then how much I would have had to suffer, my hands would have trembled as I raised the sacred host. On that summit so near to heaven I understood better the mission with which God had entrusted me. I could repeat with more conviction the words of Isaiah – 'Here I am, send me!'

There are echoes here of the experience of Jesuit Pierre Teilhard de Chardin, who on Easter Sunday, 1923, sat under a tree in the Ordos Desert of Inner Mongolia, and as the sun came up wrote a mystical essay titled *Mass on the World.*

With neither bread, nor wine, nor altar, I your priest will make the whole earth my altar and on it will offer you all the labours and sufferings of the world … Once again Fire has penetrated the Earth. No visible tremor marks this transformation; and yet, at the touch of your Word the immense host, which is the universe, is made flesh. Through your incarnation, my God, all matter is henceforth incarnate.

This theme of the universal scope of the Eucharist has penetrated deeply into Catholic thought. Pope Francis in his 2015 Encyclical *Laudato Si'* writes, making reference to Pope St John Paul II's Encyclical *Ecclesia de Eucharistia,* 'The Eucharist is an act of cosmic love: "yes, cosmic, because even when it is celebrated on the humble altar of a country church, the Eucharist is always in some way celebrated on the altar of the world"'.

For Reflection

How does Pedro's commitment to prayer touch your own heart? Do you talk over your affairs with God, as one friend speaks with another, and see that as real prayer?

Have you a hunger for the Eucharist, and can you see it as an act of cosmic love?

CHAPTER 8

PEDRO IN IRELAND

Shortly after taking office, Pedro decided to visit as many of the Jesuit provinces and missions as he could. This arduous mandate was given him by the General Congregation that had elected him. It was fulfilling for a man who wanted both to learn what the Society of Jesus was up to, and to share the spirit of The Second Vatican Council and the Congregation. He loved to dialogue with his brethren on how best to meet the emerging issues of a changing world. He visited all the continents, and each visit is a study in itself.

Ireland offers a microcosm: he came first in June 1967, to an Ireland that has now vanished. Archbishop of Dublin John Charles McQuaid had told his expectant flock on his return from the Council in 1965: 'You may have been worried by much talk of changes to come. Allow me to reassure you. No change will worry the tranquillity of your Christian lives'. There was an atmosphere of episcopal caution towards the world and towards lay initiatives. Blind faith and passivity were commended. 'Pay up, Pray up, Shut up!' became the joke of the day.

Although the crowded schedule of receptions, speeches, homilies and meals was essentially intended for meetings with the 450 Irish Jesuits, the country took notice of Pedro's arrival. He met with members of the government and the Bishops, and with Jesuit associates. President Eamon de Valera declined his invitation only because of illness.

A single media quote will be enough to catch the flavour of this three-day event. *The Irish Independent* editorial, headed 'Distinguished Visitors' says: 'It is surely a sign of the times that the Archbishop of Canterbury and the General of the Society of Jesus are visiting Ireland in the same weekend … We are clearly of interest to the Christian world beyond our shores'.

He met a confused band of Irish Jesuits. As obedient men, the elders had bought into the pre-Second Vatican Council Church; any criticism of it appeared a disloyalty. The younger men yearned for openness and inspiration but could not find it. They asked: 'Are our communities places of mutual support, understanding, acceptance and openness? If not, why stay in them?' The province that Pedro addressed was a divided one, a segment of the world-wide Society. What then had he to say to such an audience?

An eye to social justice

He had come, Pedro said, to meet with Irish Jesuits 'so that the Society I serve can serve Ireland better'. He noted appreciatively that twenty per cent of Irish Jesuits were working overseas and stressed the need for those at home to update all ministries with an eye to social justice, using the global social survey he had initiated. The Society was by preference to serve the poor, even at the price of abandoning works which were good in themselves but did not help the disadvantaged. We would, he admitted, need courage to move in this way, since truth does not please everybody. Alms are not enough: we must enable everyone we serve to develop to the fullness of their personality. It must not be said of us that 'you preach a very fine-sounding doctrine, but only the socialists and the communists have improved our condition'. He was both encouraging and challenging:

> Our Society has a great future, but we must become elastic. You have chosen in Christ to serve a world in movement that needs to be put in contact with his personality. If you stop, you say 'no', not only to the world but to Christ who goes onward with the world.

He met with parents of Jesuits and brought the mothers to tears – including my own! – when he acknowledged their generosity in giving their sons to the Society, but he left the fathers a bit miffed at the fact that *their* sacrifice was not mentioned. His soft spot for mothers was revealed when he brought back to a young Jesuit studying in Rome a message from his mother to write more often!

A time of suffering

Pedro returned to Dublin on 15 August 1971, to open the Fourth International Congress of Jesuit Ecumenists. He found time to update the province on the current state of the Society. His mood was more sombre now: he spoke of a time of Gethsemane but also of the sure hope of resurrection. Problems were to be seen as challenges; inner freedom was needed to let go the past and embrace the new horizons into which God was beckoning. While numbers had declined by 4,000, more importantly, he said, the Society was looked to with great hope and affection by Pope Paul VI.

He asked those in formation for commitment to the intellectual apostolate and to familiarity with the history of the Society. He expressed gratitude for the honest expression of differences of opinion about the health of the province. He was departing, he said, with a sense of supernatural confidence and optimism: 'If God is for us, who can be against us?'

He came again in April 1978, was warmly received, and gave addresses on the role of local superiors, on the challenges for our educational apostolate, on the role of formation and on the internationality of the Society. The following year I met him in Rome as a member of a delegation that was proposing to set up the Dublin University School of Theology: the acronym was DUST. He was enthusiastic about the initiative but reminded us as we were departing that the key factor would be the approval of the archbishop. The acronym for the project turned out to be all too accurate.

His last visit was in June 1981, when he met with all involved in formation, then with 200 of the brethren. I recall how he was at his enthusiastic best and that he made no less an impression than in 1967 when he first visited us. He blessed the site of the new nursing unit at Cherryfield Lodge in Dublin, a symbol of the phenomenon of ageing that was emerging in the province. Within two months he himself was fated to be in nursing care in Rome, never to recover.

For Reflection

When you make changes in your life, do you keep the needy in mind?

'A time of Gethsemane' – how do you cope in dark times?

CHAPTER 9

THE STRUGGLE FOR JUSTICE, 1975

The central theme of the 1971 Synod of Bishops was 'Justice in the World'. This flowed from the Second Vatican Council but demanded such a deep level of conversion by the Church that it was shelved and allowed to fade away from ecclesial consciousness. Pedro had lived through many situations of injustice, had contributed to the final session of Second Vatican Council on the role of the Church in world affairs and had followed this up forcefully in the Synod. Thus, his dream was to focus all Jesuit talent, resources and works on this single mission of justice. He worked tirelessly to gain support for this, and in 1975 the thirty-second General Congregation approved a landmark decree on *The Service of Faith and the Promotion of Justice.* The key insight was that there could be no preaching of the Gospel without working for justice. Using the image of our two hands he noted that faith is one hand and justice is the other, and we do our most constructive work when we use both. But with the Church largely unready and unwilling for this revolutionary view of evangelisation, he saw that the struggle to link faith and justice would be one of the greatest challenges to the Society.

He believed that we must learn to serve those most at risk, those whom no one else is serving, but first we must love them. Where the poor are, God is, because the poor are the friends of God. He always loved the poor and they him. He tells how after a Mass in a Latin American slum a tough burly man in the congregation said to him:

> 'Come with me and I will share something precious with you.' It was evening. We walked a distance, climbed a hill and came to the poor man's house. Then my host said: 'Sit here and see the sunset, how beautiful it is'. We watched it in silence and awe, then the man said: 'Señor, I did not know how to thank you for all that you have done for us. I have nothing to give you, but I thought you would like to see this sunset. It pleased you, didn't it? *Buenas noches!*'

It was his gift to Pedro, who saw that the poor have so much to give us and that life is not only about doing things for other people, but, as here, about being in solidarity with them, sharing in the mystery and beauty of creation.

A *Sign of Contradiction*

Conflicts around renewal and especially the promotion of justice were rife in the seventies both in the Church and in religious congregations. Bringing good news to the poor meant disturbing the status quo in which the poor were oppressed and rendered voiceless. Within the Society, conservatives and liberals became highly polarised, with both sides pressing for the values they sincerely believed in. For some the slogan was: 'This is not the Society I joined!' For others, Arrupe was the man who re-founded the Jesuits, and they rallied to him. The growth of liberation theology in Latin America was seen variously as deriving from Jesus or Marx. Opposition to Pedro's vision, to his gentle use of authority, to his openness to experimentation, to his interpretation of the Ignatian charism came from a number of bishops, and they had the ear of the three popes under whom he served: Paul Vl, John Paul I and John Paul II. Pedro became a sign of contradiction and endured the painful tensions between faithfulness to the Second Vatican Council and to the post-conciliar Church that was at best ambiguous about *aggiornamento* (bringing up to date). When a group of Spanish Jesuits came to feel in all good conscience that they should break away in order to restore the traditional Jesuit way of life, Pedro had to work hard to commend to them the authenticity of current Jesuit life, expressed though it might be in differing forms.

His critics felt that his style of government was inadequate to the challenges he faced; that his tendency to believe the best of everyone was naïve, and that he was failing to stamp out abuses. He needed, they felt, to face abuses with a firm hand rather than with persuasion; to call his troops to order and discipline the rebellious. But this was not in Pedro's character. Neither was he a diplomat as Ignatius was, nor had he spent time in his earlier years learning Roman ways. Presuming the best of everyone, he pushed ahead with the implementation of the Council's agenda without keeping clear lines of communication open with the Vatican. This was a serious, and as we shall see, a tragic one. His enthusiastic temperament and his missionary experience of the needs of humankind led him to run ahead of a Church that arrived on the platform of change somewhat breathless and a little late.

One incident will illustrate the problem: Pope Paul VI, who died in 1978, had a great reverence for the Society of Jesus: he idealised it. He called Pedro in on one occasion and read him a carefully prepared letter with twelve points. The first eleven were commendatory, the twelfth carried a strong admonition which the Pope was trying to get across to Pedro with Vatican tact and diplomacy. Pedro on returning home to the Jesuit curia announced happily: 'The Holy Father has praised our work in eleven points: only on the twelfth did he show reserve!'

The Gathering Storm

John Paul I governed for just over a month in 1978. He was, it is said, preparing a scolding letter for the Jesuits when out of the blue he died. John Cornwell's imaginative book, *A Thief in the Night: the Mysterious Death of Pope John Paul I* suggests that among other groups, the Jesuits stood to gain from the Pope's untimely death, and therefore … !

In personality and background, his successor Pope John Paul II differed radically from Pedro. They saw the world differently and effectively used different languages, so that common ground between them narrowed to vanishing point. Collegiality, promised by the Second Vatican Council, had not materialised, so the Holy See continued in its monolithic authority. Coming out of his personal experience in communist Poland the Pope had high regard for traditional Catholic ways of doing things and was trying to hold the universal Church together in the wake of the council. He was open to complaints by bishops and disaffected Jesuits to the effect that Pedro was presiding over the disruption of the Church. Pedro on the other side was an imaginative optimist who was willing to try anything good for the sake of the kingdom, and who had made the front cover of *Time* in April 1973.

Among the neuralgic issues of the time were the tension between faith and justice, liberation theology, liturgical renewal, ecumenical relations, mandatory priestly celibacy, birth control and more. While principled disagreement characterised the struggle of minds and hearts at the Second Vatican Council, the art of graced conflict was poorly understood and practised in the Church. It is significant that in John O'Malley's magisterial work, *What Happened at Vatican II*, neither 'conflict' nor 'disagreement' are listed in the index, even though, as he illustrates, every other sentence of its decrees was fought over. Attitudes towards change differed dramatically in the Church: is it a fortress, the rock of ages, or is it better imaged as a pilgrim people, a community of disciples? Was Newman right or wrong in holding that 'to live is to change, and to be perfect is to have changed often'?

The effort to reach towards the truth promised us by Jesus (Jn 16:13) is a laborious task. Conflict can be graced, however, when in the midst of disagreement it edges Christians to mutual acceptance. Community – as unity in diversity – is the resulting miracle. The challenge is 'not to kill one another in the cause of truth but to love one another in our differences'. A post-Reformation nugget of wisdom argues: 'In necessary matters there must be unity;

in doubtful ones, liberty; and in all things, charity'.

Pedro's devotion to Pope John Paul II was never in question; it had even a mystical quality. But he did not deliver what was asked of him; relations unravelled to the point that in 1980 he offered his resignation to John Paul II, on the grounds of advanced age. The pope feared that if Pedro resigned a new general might take his place who was more difficult to deal with. So he procrastinated, asking Pedro to continue for the time being. To this we shall return.

For Reflection

How do you manage conflict?

Do you continue to try to love others with whom you disagree? Do you find yourself praying for them?

CHAPTER 10

THE JESUIT REFUGEE SERVICE 1980

The year 1980 was especially difficult for Pedro but he never lost heart. This may seem so obvious as to pass unnoticed, but it says much about his spirit. He was besieged with problems on every side, both from within the Order – opposition to needed change, decline of numbers – and from within the Church at its highest levels. Also to a personality optimistic by nature the sorry state of world affairs must have been deeply challenging. He laboured on, a figure of hope to many and of irritation to others, a man full of creativity and leadership. He was inspired, with far-reaching consequences, to set up the Jesuit Refugee Service in November of that year.

Since refugee crises can break out overnight, Pedro wanted his men to be available at short notice to leave established apostolates and academic posts in order to enter into solidarity with refugees wherever they were to be found. This was in line with Ignatius's call to go where the need was greatest, and where noone else was available. From his personal knowledge through travel, he had come to see that of all the people in the world, refugees were most at risk. He was particularly shocked at the plight of the Vietnamese boat people, of whom some two million risked everything to escape repression after the Vietnam War. This was perhaps the largest exodus in modern history and the world was not prepared for it. In an Ignatian-style response to a crisis, he asked simply, 'what ought we to do?'

He shared his distress with those in leadership across the Society. 'To incarnate the Ignatian vision' he said, 'we must get ourselves out of the concrete!' His appeal struck a chord: offers came in of personnel and money; the lobbying of governments and other agencies began. That the response was so generous shows that his efforts for the renewal of the Society were bearing fruit. He stressed that those who volunteered did not have to be high-flyers:

> We are normal in that we are not geniuses. Perhaps we have a few geniuses in the Society, but very few. Years ago it was said that the great power the Society possesses is its well-trained mediocrity! Real excellence lies in commitment to Christ. Everything must be done with great discernment.

The JRS has become a dramatic symbol of what the Society of Jesus is meant to be, and also inspires many lay people to abandon the predictable and safe in order to serve the unwanted of the world, of which there are perhaps 70 million.

He made an exhausting visit to the Philippines in July

1981, in which he presided at fourteen Eucharists and gave twenty-six addresses, always with the same inspiring and challenging message about availability to serve people through faith and justice, but in a way that is 'rooted and grounded in love'.

What proved to be his final exhortation was an impromptu address to those working with refugees in Thailand. It is a call to interiority.

> Please, be brave! I will tell you one more thing and please don't forget it! Pray, pray much. The problems we have been discussing will not be resolved by human power. I am saying to you something that I want to underline, a message, perhaps my swan song for the Society! In our three-day meetings, if we spend half a day in prayer about the conclusions we expect to come to, we will have very different inspirations. We will come to quite different syntheses, ones we could never find in books nor arrive at through discussion. If we are at the forefront of a new apostolate, we must be illuminated by the Holy Spirit. These are not the pious words of a novice master: what I am saying is 100% Ignatian! We must have a basic union of minds for this new apostolate which is being born. Now we are going through the birth pangs! From this medical point of view I come to the end of my talk!

He was speaking on the thirty-sixth anniversary of Hiroshima. The following day, 7 August 1981, on his return to Rome, he suffered a massive stroke that left him partially paralysed and with severely impaired speech.

1981 until 1991. Increasingly unable to communicate, he grew feeble and suffered much inner darkness. Though almost mute, he could follow what was said to him, and he who had been such a busy traveller and so articulate about the Society's response to global issues, was marginalised and confined to a single room in semi-darkness. His formal resignation in 1983, read to his brethren at the thirty-third Congregation, reflects the indomitable spirit of a physically broken man:

> More than ever I find myself in the hands of God. This is what I have wanted all my life from my youth. But now there is a difference: the initiative is entirely with God. It is indeed a profound spiritual experience to know and feel myself so totally in God's hands.

These final words were received with thunderous applause and with silent tears. They continue to inspire many whose lives have fallen apart and who find themselves lost in a strange and barren land. Can we say something of what goes on there? Teilhard speaks of the divinising of our passivities – the things over which we have little control. All we can do is accept them patiently and with bone-hard love. Jesuit Gerard Manley Hopkins notes 'those years and years of world without event' as shaping the greatness of the Jesuit door-keeper St Alphonsus Rodriguez. God's grace, we can believe, operates not only in fruitfulness but in failure and inability, though its path is over rocky ground and hard to trace. But Jesus promised that 'your endurance will win you your lives' (Lk 21:19). The self-emptying of Jesus was completed in death; only when the grain of wheat died did God raise him up in glory. So for Pedro: like Peter before him he was taken to a place to which he 'would rather not go'. Miserable it was, yet he found God there before him.

A tiny incident catches the pain of his forced inactivity and silence. A friend who had called on him said as his visit was ending, 'Sorry I have to go now, Pedro'. 'Ah, you have to go' whispered Pedro. What he would have given to be able to say these words! This desolate decade of a life of extraordinary dedication and generosity mercifully came to a close on 5 February 1991. He was eighty-three years old.

Reconciliation

Was the rift between Pope John Paul II and Pedro healed before he died? We know that within three weeks of Pedro's stroke the Pope wrote him a letter of sympathy, noting that he himself was convalescing after his attempted assassination. Writing in Polish the Pope expressed the hope that, like himself, Pedro would recover and that together 'they would carry forward, in the way that God wills, the cause which God has entrusted to our human weakness'.

When the Pope wrote to say that he was bypassing those who would normally have taken over the governing of the Society, he closed his devastating letter with a message of goodwill:

> I trust that the Society of Jesus will recognise in these decisions a sign of my affectionate regard for you and of my sincere goodwill for the whole Society, having very much at heart its greater good, which will redound to the advantage of the whole Church, in which the Society carries out such a vast and varied ministry.

The Pope is said to have admitted later in private that he

had feared a rebellion following on this decision but was greatly impressed by the response of the Society, and that he had been badly informed about the quality of their obedience. We know that some days before Pedro died, the Pope visited him and gave him his apostolic blessing; this was a huge comfort to the dying man, given his reverence for the papacy. Doubtless more will be brought to light on the relationship between the two men when the petition for Pedro's beatification is complete.

For Reflection

When you visit an incapacitated or dying person, do you experience a sense of that mystery which Pedro describes as 'being in the hands of God'?

Are you a forgiving person? If so, how do you show it?

CHAPTER 12

A DEMANDING LEGACY

Most of what Jesuits and their partners in mission do is hidden, but the legacy is also written in blood, because the struggle for faith and justice is carried out under the cross and leads to conflict with dominant and powerful opponents. Pedro wrote a reflective letter in 1977 on the killing of five Jesuits within a few months of each other, in places as far apart as El Salvador, Brazil and Zimbabwe.

> These are the Jesuits which the world and the Church needs today. Men impelled by the love of Christ, who serve their sisters and brothers without distinction of race or class. Men who know how to identify with those who suffer, how to live with them to the point of giving their lives to help them. Brave men who know how to defend human rights to the extreme of sacrificing their lives, if it be necessary.

There had followed soon after a threat by the government-assisted death squads of El Salvador: 'We will kill all forty-seven Jesuits if they do not leave the country now!' To which Pedro replied: 'They may end up as martyrs, but they are not going to leave, because they are with the people of El Salvador'. He had got the unanimous consent of his brethren before making this reply.

It is a stark reality that more than fifty Jesuits from twenty countries have died violently on mission since the Jesuits committed themselves explicitly to promote faith and justice as the twin dimensions of the Gospel message. The Arrupe legacy, then, is not for the faint of heart. It is for those who know themselves to be weak but who, like Pedro, put themselves into God's hands and let God lead them. May his inspiration continue to fire many to a similar generosity.

Should he be canonised? Jesuits do not tend to get carried away by canonisations. But he witnessed in an extraordinary way to the disturbing freshness of Christ. We can apply to him a wise comment by Emmanuel Cardinal Suhard, Archbishop of Paris during the Second World War:

> To be a witness does not consist in engaging in propaganda, nor even in stirring people up, but in being a living mystery. It means to live in such a way that one's life would not make sense if God did not exist.

For millions of people across the world, Pedro is such 'a living mystery'. Across the globe, and most importantly in its poorer areas, schools, educational centres, refugee facilities, hostels for the homeless and so forth, have been named after him. The Jesuit Refugee Service, less than forty years old, spans the globe, with more than 1500 members in 50 countries. Pedro's vision has aptly been termed 'a mysticism of history'; historical mysticism turns towards the chaos and messiness of concrete events. It is a mysticism of active service. It takes on a responsibility for those who are suffering, whether in the aftermath of Hiroshima or in tiny boats escaping on the high seas from Vietnam.

There is no reason to believe that Pedro's capacity to inspire will weaken. Through his labour to recover the original dynamism of Ignatian spirituality, he continues to enrich the lives of millions. In his lifetime Pedro engendered an intense loyalty and affection, and he does so still. Pope Francis as a Jesuit owes much to him – he shares Pedro's vision of the world as the place where we encounter God. I like to believe that from his new vantage-point he can see the seeds he planted with so much industry-bearing fruit a hundredfold.

Unlike him we may not make the front cover of *Time* magazine but that matters little. Our lives can be filled with meaning through falling in love with God as he did, living the rest of our days in companionship with his Son, and serving his people in whatever ways are shown to us. The following lines, attributed to Pedro, catch the point with startling clarity:

> Nothing is more practical than finding God,
> that is, than falling in love in an absolute, final
>   way.
> What you are in love with,
> what seizes your imagination,
> will affect everything.
> It will decide what will get you out of bed in
>   the mornings,

what you will do with your evenings,
how you spend your weekends,
what you read, who you know, what breaks
   your heart,
and what amazes you with love and gratitude.
Fall in love, stay in love, and it will decide
   everything!'

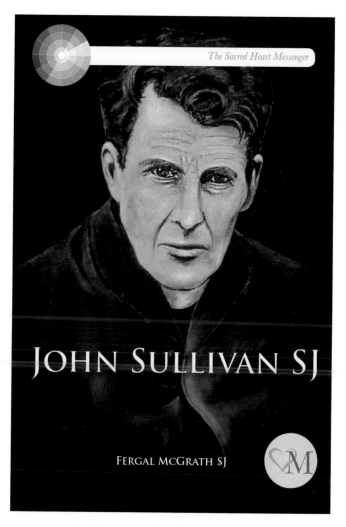

The Sacred Heart Messenger

JOHN SULLIVAN SJ

FERGAL McGRATH SJ

WWW.MESSENGER.IE
TEL: 01 7758522
€3.99

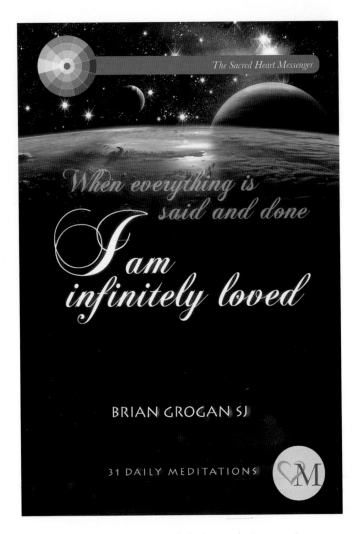

The Sacred Heart Messenger

When everything is
said and done

*I am
infinitely loved*

BRIAN GROGAN SJ

31 DAILY MEDITATIONS

WWW.MESSENGER.IE
TEL: 01 7758522
€4.95